Atlantic International University
A New Age for Distance Learning

ROBERT D. BENDA

ID #: UM32356BPR40930

PROJECT PORTFOLIO MANAGEMENT

PORTFOLIO MANAGEMENT: AN APPROACH TO REDUCING RISK AND IMPROVING
ORGANIZATIONAL STRATEGIES IN THE FIELD OF PROJECT MANAGEMENT

ATLANTIC INTERNATIONAL UNIVERSITY
HONOLULU, HAWAII

DECEMBER 2014

Atlantic International University
A New Age for Distance Learning

TABLE OF CONTENTS

1.0 INTRODUCTION

Project portfolio management has become very important and also serves as core function in many organizations. Projects are any temporary activities that have starting and finish date; it has performance parameters which can be determined by the project portfolio. Projects face triple constrains to include (A) time (B) budget and (C) performance. It was assumed that for attainment of organizational goals one has to meet triple constraints of time, budget and performance. It is at this point that Project portfolio management plays a vital role in achieving organizational goals and considered as backbone of organization. Project portfolio management is a knowledge that meets the requirements of projects as it is crucial in project implementation and execution. Project portfolio management plays important role in accomplishing project strategies, business goals and desired outcomes. Organizations link their projects with their

portfolio management strategies to achieve the anticipated goals and objectives. Portfolio management Strategies are activities that guide and direct the use of the resources to accomplish the organization's vision and goals and sustainable competitive advantage. Mostly these components comprising the strategies of the business like internal analysis, organizational structures, control systems have strong links to project management processes and activities.

Therefore, this paper examines Project Portfolio Management as an approach to reducing risk and improving strategies in the field of project management.   It further depicts that Project portfolio management is a precise method to diminish risk in the implementation of projects for the reason that it purposes to accomplish achievement and breach the gap between strategy making and implementation thereby connecting them together. This paper argues that there is a lot of significance of project portfolio

management in assessing, highlighting and choosing projects in with relation to organizational strategy.

This paper defines Project Portfolio Management as an approach to selecting the genuine projects and vital fragment of strategic management in organizations for impact. Project portfolio management outlines the technique or stratagem in which a project management team resolves to participate in the market as compared to other contenders and cessations the breach of these approaches with project portfolio management.

Keywords: Project portfolio management, project management, organizational strategies, and alignment.

2.0 DESCRIPTION

Project portfolio management is all about risk and profit making strategies. Portfolio management is apprehensive with the organizing

and management of assets. There are two principal schools of thought regarding project portfolio management: reflexive and dynamic. A reflexive and dynamic term refers to the method by which the assets are selected for inclusion into the portfolio. A reflexive portfolio includes the market portfolio; consist of shares in all companies quoted on the stock exchange, or a selection of group of stock e.g. all technology stocks. A reflexive portfolio consequently does not make any effort to make inquiry about routine and agree if it ought to be comprised or omitted from the organization project portfolio. There is no practical or ultimate investigation accepted in order to worn out the general project portfolio. Reflexive equity portfolio management is totally about long-term acquisition and hold strategy within a certain time frame. It aim is to be level with the organization's portfolio expectation **(Sanwal, Anand 2007)**.

Dynamic portfolio management on the other hand uses research, analysis which is both essential and procedural; it also involves an economic factor and also an element of subjective judgment in selecting stock into the project portfolio. It is believed that the stocks are undervalued and will outperform the market portfolio in the future.

Project portfolio management has become very important topic all over the world. Previous literature shows that many establishments fail to accomplish its project's goals with success due to misalignment between their professional strategies and project management. Many organizations face this problem of missing link of business strategies and project management. Alignment is necessary for getting competitive advantage and goals of its business. Top management also play important role in alignment of professional strategies and Project portfolio management.

4.0   GENERAL ANALYSIS

Project portfolio management is a practice refers to the identification of a project investment categorization scheme to assist the organization with prioritizing projects.

Project portfolio management forms one of the building blocks in relating projects to strategy and can be considered as a key driver for aligning projects or programs to organizational objectives **(Rao 2007).**

Project management comprises of project portfolio management. Project Portfolio Management is about how organizations controls theirs projects and align them with business strategies. Many organizations are working on numerous projects and they are conscious to get concentrated outcomes. Project Portfolio Management also

surrounds the increase of project yields which is the overall objective of all organizations. Basically, projects are the foundations of any organization to build up their business/project strategy. When organizations aligned their projects to their organization's business strategy, they are improved and able to achieve their organizational goals. Establishments must align their organizational professional strategy with the project management feat to device the strategies in their projects implementation. These alignments are challenging since their goals and approach are erstwhile not vibrant and interconnected with project management. Misalignment them might cause an organization to miss it project goals, cause a breach in communication and miss-link their organizational business strategy and project management practices. The lack of alignment of the organization's strategy to the project management leads to the project failure and has adverse effects on organization performance as well. There is need of systemic approach to align the projects with the organization's

strategy. So important in managerial challenges involved aligning project management and business strategy and encouraging individuals to participate in using emerging strategies to create new ideas and renew existing strategies.

Some factors help in creating a link between organizational strategy and project management if there is any gap between the bridge of organization's strategy and project portfolio management that should be filled to achieve high returns and competitive advantages. Some rudiments such as spirit, strategy, organization, tools and processes can be aligned between the organization's strategies and project portfolio management in depth of understanding the factors that are missing and the relationship of these factors with the organization's strategies and project portfolio management. Project Portfolio management plays important role in project management and other business strategy linking. Implementation of strategies with formulation, receive less

attention than formulation so there should be proper emphasis on the implementation as well as. Organizational strategy describes the way in which a firm decides to compete in the market compared to its competitors and close the gap of these strategies with project portfolio management.

4.0 ACTUALIZATION

Successful initiation of projects and its execution mostly depends upon the organization's portfolio management quality and its strategies. Many organizations in the field of project management are suffering from misaligned projects and a lack of a systematic portfolio management approach to align project management with the organization's strategy. When organizations link their projects to their

strategies, they are better able to accomplish their organizational goals. Project strategy should be related to the projects goals and objectives in order to attain the preferred position in its competitive environment.

4.1 Organizational Strategy

Strategy can be well-defined as a complete customary of activities which guide and direct the use of the organization's resources to achieve the organization's visualization and objectives and permit sustainable reasonable benefit. Turning strategy into action to operationalize strategic objectives to achieve competitive advantage includes in the strategic management. Several scholars suggest that the success of project should be considered in the context of the achievement of the strategic goals of the organization and that organizations are better able to accomplish their goals when they link their projects to their business strategy **(Kenny, 2006).**

To ensure strategies are translated into actions they should be operational and includes some of the characteristics like organizing an organization to support effective performance and allowing achievement via various resource areas like individuals, information, funding, etc. of an organization. Better implementation of strategic plans results in the better performance of development, retributions deposits and growth on the overall invested capital than those organization that do not implement their strategic plans.

However, in any organization there are different levels of strategies presented by different level of a business which includes Corporate Strategy: It involves high level of strategic decision making and purpose of this strategy is to achieve the expectations of the stakeholders. Operational Strategy: It's concerned with the coordination and improvement of resources which results in the effective and efficient implementation of the business unit level strategy. Implementation of

strategies entails conducting project activities to implement tasks, and concentrate on the realization of these strategies.

4.2 Aligning Organizational Strategy and Project Portfolio Management

Decision-making challenges involve aligning project management and organizational strategy which encourages persons to play a part in expending developing strategies to produce firsthand concepts and reintroduce prevailing approaches. There is no such research regarding the framework for aligning project management and organizational strategy systematically. The literature has highlighted that there are numerous projects which must be implemented without implementing the organization's strategies as it has been framed by managers in the organization's level short of the participation of the project manager.

Aligning the organization's projects to make the most of their influences to strategic objectives takes an extremely organized effort.

Amalgamation involves a practice for highlighting projects by their impact to the strategic blueprint. For organizations to developed into a more competitive one to be well-organized and profitable, they will need a professional and project managing specialists functioning together to accomplish the organization's project objectives. Aligning organizational strategy and project portfolio management is a major concern for any organization. These alignments can be thought-provoking since their objectives and their strategy are not constantly perfect or communicated well or dependable through project management activities. Misalignment can affect an organization to miss goals and objectives. . It decreases danger and advances the organizational strategies in the field of project management. Considering the arrangement might be one of the major encounters to operative project management procedure (**Jonas, D. 2010**).

5.0   DISCUSSIONS

Project portfolio management implementation necessitates an organizational arrangement which supports projects. Consequently, organizations need a project miscellany and primacy method in a bid to guarantee sturdy connections between projects and the strategic blueprint. Project portfolio management processes comprise of scheduling, implementing, and regulating. These are vital to safeguard that we are able to implement strategies effectively and efficiently for success. Implementing this effort entails apportionment of assets such as capitals, individuals, and paraphernalia. Organizational resources are

restricted while Project portfolio management Implementation needs to contain consideration to the succeeding crucial arguments:

5.1 Organizational Portfolio Preparation/Scheduling

The preparation/scheduling stage of project portfolio management embroils a transcribed asset program declaration. This obviously well-defined asset strategy contains the ideal management procedure, hereafter, dynamic or reflexive portfolio management. This also summaries the portfolio objectives and defines tolerances for the portfolio. The preparation/scheduling encompass corresponding strategies and resources of the organization to achieve its interior and exterior communication objectives.

5.2 Organizational Portfolio Quality Analysis, Assortment and Amalgamation

Quality assortment management is grounded on dual types of asset analysis: technical analysis and fundamental analysis. Technical analysis is centered on reviewing past tendencies in share values with the confidence that frameworks can be distinguished in their activities which can be used to envisage impending activities. Fundamental analysis focuses on the revision of the fundamental position of the organization. These details can be used as its strengths and weaknesses and imminent prospects and intimidations, likewise practices proportion investigation in appraising a specific standard.

In quality assortment and amalgamation, we need to remember that projects are risk-adverse and they must be assorted by their portfolios by the mean of quality. However, quality amalgamation does result in an increase portfolio returns as a result of how the projects are amalgamated and allocated within the available quality classes.

5.3 Assessment of Project Portfolio Recital

Portfolio recital assessment includes reoccurrence quantity completed over several times. Recital methods like project scheduling and safety investigation are all significant to project portfolio management. Style appraisal is often used to designate a portfolio by appraising by what means its profits performance is, rather than by expending a one-dimensional perception of whatsoever the portfolio encompassed. Its objective is also to make available a higher mean of recital quantity for the proficiency of the account manager.

The changing aspects are profit concerns involving to the portfolio as there are numerous methods available to consider the performance of a portfolio. Style examination is one of the latest available methods and it permits project managers and organizations to elucidate by what means project portfolio yields perform.

5.4 Reflexive   and Dynamic Portfolios

Today, there are several rewards of reflexive portfolio management over that of dynamic portfolio. I have already deliberated and proposed that dynamic management has very little importance in relations to portfolio assortment and selection in project management efficiency. So reflexive portfolio management costs is much less than that of dynamic portfolio management and this provides reflexive portfolio an upturn net yields as the management costs are lower. Reflexive reciprocated funds have a characteristically low turnover of safeties and thus are exposed to fewer realized project gains.

A dynamic portfolio is one that is not reflexive. Dynamic portfolio manager's portfolio will vary from that of a reflexive manager. This is because dynamic managers will act on awareness of mispricing in project management process, and as such perceptions change frequently, such managers tend to craft frequently.

Dynamic portfolio manager's perils are minor than that of reflexive managers, due to the high cost of vigorously handling the portfolio. If the projects deliverables are semi-strong or strong form efficient, then dynamic portfolio management in relations to important or technical analysis are waste of time as they will not deliver any possible achievements in determining the projects underrated deliverables. Therefore, dynamic portfolio management is a fruitless implementation and can lead to waste of both resources and funds (**Rajegopal, Shan; Philip McGuin; James Waller 2007**).

Reflexive portfolios have predictable styles. A reflexive project manager knows exactly what types of safeties he or she is financed in a bid to decrease risks. Dynamic project managers, on the other side, can show a discrepancy from the alignment of their portfolios meaningfully within a particular time interval.

6.0 GENERAL RECOMMENDATIONS

Let me summarize here that Project portfolio management is essential and the prioritization of projects management. Project portfolio selection depends on being capable to bond and highlight projects according to an understanding of what the capability of an organization is relative to other organizations.

However, I wish to suggest and recommend the following for consideration:

➢ That project portfolio management be utilized as an approach to reducing risk and improving organizational strategies in the field of project management;

➢ That projects selection and approval should be based on competency building and quality of their organizational portfolios rather than traditional financial analysis; and

> Organizations must implement specific projects that are in alignment with their strategic goals for their success rate to rise intensely because exclusive funding would not be an problem.

7.0 CONCLUSION: A NEW PERSPECTIVE

This paper explores the contribution of project portfolio management in the field of project management as it relates to reducing risk and improving organizational strategies. It is based on the four basic strategies I proposed to include: organizational portfolio preparation/scheduling, organizational portfolio quality analysis, assortment and amalgamation, assessment of project portfolio recital and lastly, reflexive and dynamic Portfolios.

As for the research work established in this paper, it is important to reference that the foremost concerns of this work are the misalignment between project management and professional strategy and how it occur. The concerns possibly comprise of communication regarding the project manager and project team competence concerning the Project Portfolio Management and the project team in the strategy development, manager's obligation, training and inspiration, and personal principles and countless others which lead to tie the project to the strategy. Latest investigation discoveries from Professional development designers disclosed that many organizations around the world foremost cause for project catastrophe is that most organizations do not certify that all projects they managed are arrange in a line with their organization's fundamental strategies.

Nevertheless, latest discoveries revealed that the bulk of projects on the go are not linked with the organizational strategic plans. As a result

of this, several establishments do not possess the ability to carry on the process of highlighting projects with a strong portfolio management strategy aligned with their organization. Consequently, it is not unexpected that project disappointment are proliferating as a result because senior project managers are not at the wheel to offer supervision, guidance and management to projects contained by their organization's portfolio. These organizations have no organized method in tight to highlight projects or bond them to their organization's strategic goals and objectives. The minute portfolio management is done effectively; it tries to provide excess outcomes over the reflexive portfolio by actively predicting forthcoming profits on the organizational frameworks. Nonetheless, in truth they do not gain substantial superfluous profit of the project portfolio, the main indexing for the reflexive portfolio management.

8.0 REFERENCES

Jonas, D. (2010). *Empowering project portfolio managers: How management involvement impacts project portfolio management performance.* International Journal of Project Management, 28(8), 818-831.

Kenny, J. (2006). *Strategy and the learning organization: a maturity model for the formation of strategy.* The Learning Organization, 13 (4), 353-36.

Rajegopal, Shan; Philip McGuin; James Waller (2007). *Project Portfolio Management: Leading the Corporate Vision.* Basingstoke: Palgrave Macmillan.

Rao, M. (2007). *Steering Project Success – Simple Innovations in Execution*. New York: McGraw Hill.

Sanwal, Anand (2007). *Optimizing Corporate Portfolio management: Aligning Investment Proposals with Organizational Strategy*. Wiley.

www.ingramcontent.com/pod-product-compliance
Lightning Source LLC
Chambersburg PA
CBHW041618180526
45159CB00002BC/904

* 9 7 8 1 5 0 5 3 7 2 4 5 8 *